THE WATCHMAN

Timothy Callender

HEINEMANN EDUCATIONAL BOOKS
LONDON   KINGSTON   PORT OF SPAIN

Heinemann Educational Books Ltd
22 Bedford Square, London WC1B 3HH
175 Mountain View Avenue, Kingston 6,
Jamaica
27 Belmont Circular Road, Port of Spain,
Trinidad

IBADAN NAIROBI EDINBURGH MELBOURNE
AUCKLAND HONG KONG SINGAPORE
KUALA LUMPUR NEW DELHI

Heinemann Educational Books Inc.
4 Front Street, Exeter, New Hampshire
03833, USA

© Timothy Callender 1984
First published 1984

**British Library Cataloguing in Publication
Data**

Callender, Timothy
  The Watchman — (Caribbean readers)
  1. English language — Text-books for
  foreign speakers
  I. Title II. Series
  428.2'4 PE1128

ISBN 0-435-98141-2

Cover illustration by Jeff Carter

Printed in Great Britain by BAS Printers Ltd
Over Wallop, Hampshire, UK

The morning sunlight struck its **GOLDEN BRILLIANCE** against the worn, unpainted wooden planks of a lonely chattel house, somewhere in Codrington, St. Michael, **BARBADOS**.

A gentle rising breeze fanned the coconut palms until their long leaves whispered over the roof of the shelter. The last cock crowed and fell silent.

BRIGHT and **WARM** though the sunlight was, and **TRANQUIL** the wind, there was **DARKNESS**, **COLD** and **TURMOIL** shut tight within that home.

THE WATCHMAN

Part 1

STORY, LAYOUT AND LETTERING BY TIMOTHY CALLENDER

CAST OF CHARACTERS
LIZA: SUZANNE KING
YOUNG SON: OKOLO CALLENDER
PATSY: LORNA ALETHEA CALLENDER
CEDRIC: DESMOND (FOWL) WEEKES } THE DRAYTONS TWO
TOBIAS: LEW (ZORRO) DRAYTON }
MR. SMITH: ANDY TAITT
SHARK: ROOSEVELT (TY) KING
SARGEANT ROCK: VERN BEST { EL VERNO DEL CONGO
DREADLOCKSMAN: MARK (IKANOR) BIGNALL
DIRECTED BY TIMOTHY CALLENDER

INSIDE THE SIMPLE DWELLING, A WORRIED, SAD WOMAN BRUSHED A HAND WEARILY ACROSS HER FACE. THERE WERE MANY PRESSURES ON THIS POOR WOMAN, BUT THE MOST SERIOUS PROBLEM WAS HER SICK CHILD.

SHE SAT ON THE BED AND TOUCHED THE INFANT.
THE CHILD GAZED DREAMILY INTO VACANT SPACE. ALL NIGHT IT HAD COUGHED AND WHEEZED, AND

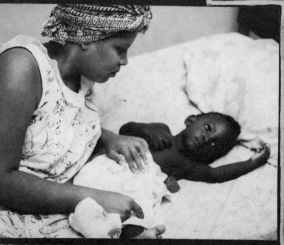  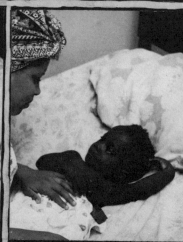

A HOT FEVER BURNT ITS TINY BODY. NOW IT TOUCHED ITS HEAD WITH A LISTLESS HAND, AND ATTEMPTED A SMILE AT ITS MOTHER.

THEN...

KNOCK-KNOCK!

PATSY!

I GLAD TO SEE YOU.

WAIT. LEMME OPEN THE DOOR.

COME IN, NUH?

BUT I ONLY GIVE YOU A CALL. I CAN'T STOP NOW, LIZA.

NOT EVEN FOR A MINUTE?

NO. BUT LIZA, YUH LOOK TIRED.

PHOTOGRAPHS BY
TONY LYNCH
ROOSEVELT 'TY' KING
TIMOTHY CALLENDER

SON'S PLAYMATES:
AISHA KING
STELLA HACKETT

PHOTOGRAPHIC PROCESSING:
TONY LYNCH, ROOSEVELT 'TY' KING

AND AS SHE HEARD PATSY'S FOOTSTEPS DIE AWAY, LIZA SAT DOWN AND STARTED TO WEEP...

UNTIL ANOTHER KNOCK SOUNDED OUTSIDE THE HOUSE.

WITH RESPECTFUL THANKS TO KING DYAL WHO ALLOWED US HIS PHOTOGRAPH

CEDRIC MOVED ON, UP RIVER ROAD AND BEYOND. IN TIME HE STOOD BEFORE ONE GATE OF A HUGE SPRAWLING LUMBERYARD. IT WAS WELL SECURED, WITH WALLS AND WIRE. PILES OF LUMBER LAY IN THIS VAST LUMBERYARD, NUMEROUS AS

MATCHSTICKS.

...WONDER WHERE THE OFFICE IS.

CEDRIC PUSHED THE BIG WOODEN GATE OPEN AND ENTERED THE LUMBERYARD. HE FELT THAT SUCH PLACES ALWAYS NEEDED A MAN OR TWO. HE LOOKED AROUND, SAW A DOOR WITH A SIGN MARKED "OFFICE", WALKED OVER, AND KNOCKED.

MR. SMITH, OF SMITH, SMITH AND JONES LTD., LISTENED CAREFULLY TO CEDRIC'S PLEAS FOR A JOB.

KNOCK-KNOCK!

COME IN.

I THINK HE'D WORK FAIRLY CHEAPLY.

I WONDER IF HE COULD GUARD THE WHOLE LUMBERYARD.

IT WOULD BE NICE IF HE COULD DO IT.

CEDRIC SOON STOPPED THINKING ABOUT SHARK AND TOBIAS.

HE WAS ON THE JOB THE NEXT EVENING, STARTING AT FOUR O'CLOCK. AT THE END OF A WEEK'S WORK HE RECEIVED HIS FIRST WAGES FROM MR. SMITH. HE TOOK THE MONEY HOME. THOUGH IT WASN'T MUCH, LIZA USED IT WELL.

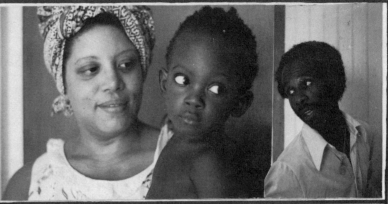

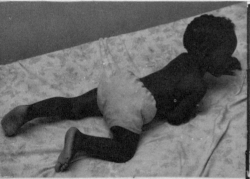

HEY.

EY.

HAHA!

THEY HAD ENOUGH TO EAT, AND THE CHILD RESPONDED WELL TO THE MEDICINE LIZA BOUGHT — OR PERHAPS THE **BUSH-TEA** WORKED. SOON IT WAS STRONG ENOUGH TO ENJOY THE SURPRISES OF FRIENDSHIP.

CEDRIC EVEN MANAGED TO MAKE A PAYMENT ON A SECONDHAND **BICYCLE** TO RIDE TO WORK.

I GETTING **BIGGER** AND **STRONGER** EVERY DAY.

SOON I GOING HAVE A REAL **BOAT**.

THEIR HOME LIFE WAS SIMPLE AND HAPPY, AND CEDRIC WAS CONTENT.

End of Part I

THE WATCHMAN Part 2

One evening, two weeks after he had taken the watchman job, Cedric was at his workplace. He sat outside the watchman house, half-dozing, for he had been working hard at home most of the day, and he was tired.

His radio was going, and the music lulled his mind.

Then, suddenly, he heard a racket at one of the lumberyard gates.

Cedric jumped up, startled, seized his cowskin whip, a stick and a rockstone, and went to make a check.

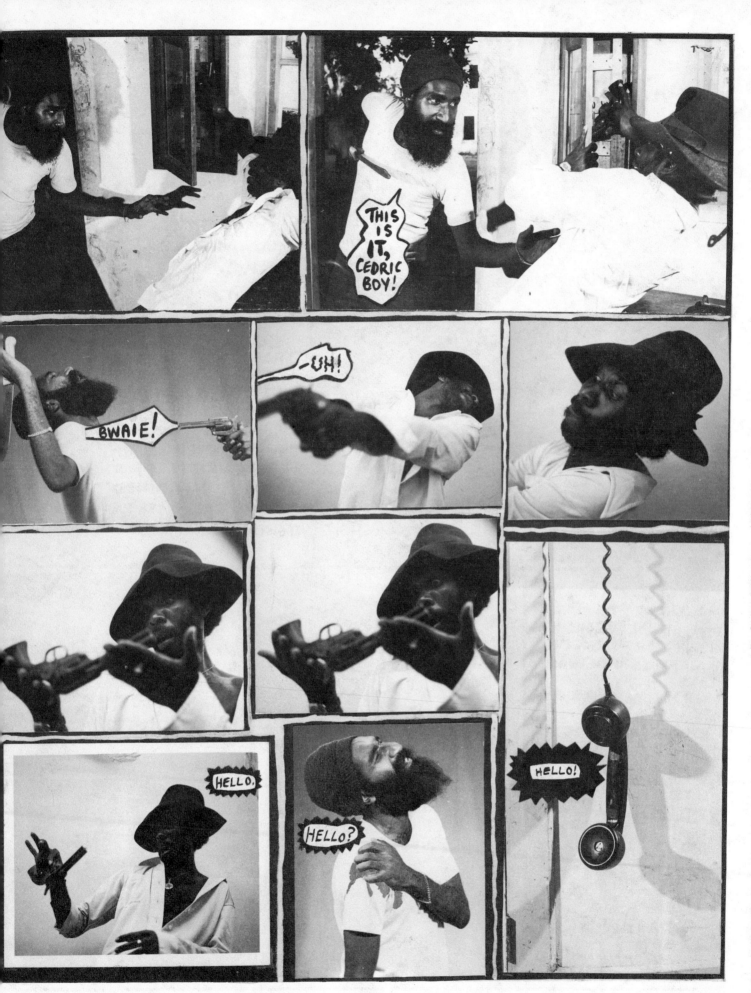

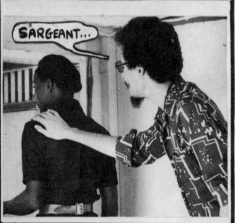

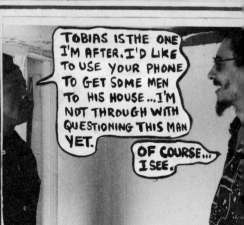

MEANWHILE — WHAT OF TOBIAS?

GOTTA GET AWAY — THEY'LL BE LOOKING FOR ME.

I HEAR A SHOT JUST NOW. WONDER IF SHARK DEAD.

IF I HAD THE TIME...

I WOULD SETTLE WITH CEDRIC.

ZOOM!

A DOUBLE HORSE-CART, WITH FRONT WHEELS CHAINED, WAS SLOWING TOBIAS'S PROGRESS. HE SWERVED TO OVERTAKE; IMMEDIATELY THE TRUCK RAN OFF THE ROAD INTO A SMALL GULLY. TOBIAS ABANDONED THE TRUCK.

HAD TO LEAVE IT ANYHOW...

...IT WAS STOLEN.

GOTTA GET HOME...

THROUGH BACKYARDS, OVER PALINGS, AND DOWN THE DIM ALLEYS AND BACKSTREETS OF THE CITY TOBIAS RACED.

19

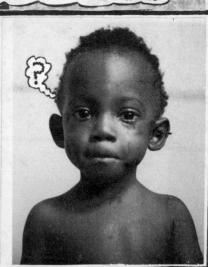

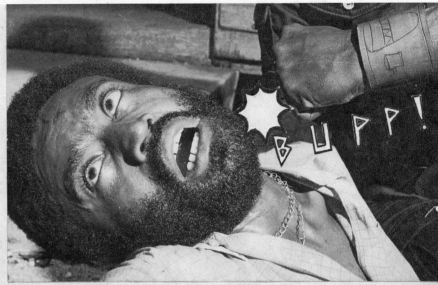

THE WATCHMAN'S SON HAD **WATCHED** THE WHOLE AFFAIR; AND SUDDENLY HE SEEMED **WISER**. **HOW** WOULD THIS EVENT AFFECT HIS **FUTURE IDEAS**?

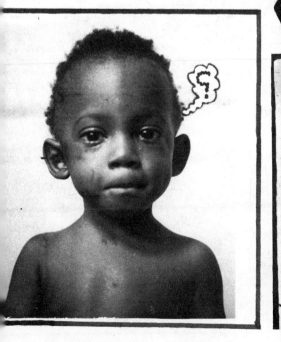

DON'T MIND HE. HE CAN'T DO WE **NUTTEN**. HE **BAD**— HE AIN'T NICE LIKE **YOU**.

Then Cedric arrived home on his bicycle, panting, for he had been riding hard and fast. The excitement was nearly over...

...though he was in time to see Tobias hustled into a police vehicle and driven away.

"I wish you two all the best."
"You're a brave woman."
"Boy - have a nice life."

Sargeant Rock, having congratulated Cedric and Liza for their help in apprehending two dangerous men, said goodbye and drove off.

And Cedric Brathwaite, free from threat and already enjoying his security and responsibility, now had the chance to improve life for his family and himself, and to know **Contentment and Prosperity**.

The End